S0-BLM-858

WITHDRAWN
UTSA Libraries

*The Flight
from Creation*

The Flight from Creation

Gustaf Wingren

Augsburg Publishing House

Minneapolis, Minnesota

THE FLIGHT FROM CREATION

Copyright © 1971 Augsburg Publishing House

Library of Congress Catalog Card No. 79-135232

International Standard Book No. 0-8066-1114-6

All rights reserved. No part of this book may be used or reproduced in any manner whatsoever without written permission except in the case of brief quotations embodied in critical articles and reviews. For information address Augsburg Publishing House, 426 South Fifth Street, Minneapolis, Minnesota 55415.

LIBRARY
University of Texas
At San Antonio

MANUFACTURED IN THE UNITED STATES OF AMERICA

Contents

Preface 7

1 **Creation: A Crucial Article of Faith** 13
My Selection of Topics

2 **Creation and Ethics** 33
From *Ordnungstheologie* to the
Theology of Revolution

3 **Creation and Theology** 57
Theology between Dogmatics and Analysis

4 **Return to Creation** 79

Notes 87

Preface

These four chapters on "The Flight from Creation" were written in different connections. They are unified positively by the first article of the Apostles' Creed, about the creation, which runs as a strong under-current in them all. Since the first article of faith is generally neglected in modern theology, the four chapters are also unified negatively by the criticism of contemporary theologians.

The first chapter is a review of my publications since 1939 and is called "Creation: A Crucial Article of Faith." Swedish systematic theology has had an historical approach and contains, for example, many reaffirmations of Luther. I entered into this Swedish tradition and have among other things published books on Irenaeus and Luther. But even when choosing historical topics of this kind I made my selection

7

of early sources with the first article of faith in mind. When Irenaeus fights the Gnostics, and when Luther puts worldly labor before the life of the cloister and celibacy, belief in the creation plays an important part in their arguments.

During the 1950s and 60s I went more directly into systematics, especially in the two books *Creation and Law* and *Gospel and Church*. It is easy to trace the inner connection back to Irenaeus and Luther. Salvation is *recapitulatio,* that is, the restoration of the creation, regained health. The church as a church is turned outwards towards the world. Its function is to protect whatever has been created from the forces that destroy life.

The second chapter takes a look at the continent of Europe and the various forms of theology that have succeeded one another there since the First World War. The first article is largely absent from this theology. One exception is the German *Ordnungstheologie* of the 1930s which spoke directly about creation and orders of creation. This is without doubt one reason why the first article fell into disuse; it had been "compromised."

When theology was again forced to include political problems on its agenda, during the latter part of the 1960s, most people were very careful to avoid mentioning "the creation." In those instances where, in spite of this, there has been a positive attitude towards revolution, it has usually been achieved through the second article, from the gospel stories about Jesus.

Statements about Jesus as a "revolutionary," which are highly dubious from the historical point of view, appear in this so-called theology of revolution.

I can only conclude, however, that the article about the creation was misinterpreted in the German *Ordnungstheologie* of the 1930s. Theologians should certainly criticize this brand of theology but they, for their own part, should not shy away from the language of the creation story, a simple, biblical, and still usable language. National socialism's misuse of the concept does not provide a reasonable explanation for the behavior of contemporary theology. Somewhere in the background there seems to be an animosity to the body and the natural manifestations of life. I am convinced that Søren Kierkegaard, among others, is responsible for this strange "illwill against nature" that is a mark of contemporary theology.

Another Dane, K. E. Løgstrup from Aarhus, has taught me more about this Kierkegaardian feature of our culture than I knew previously. I therefore mention Løgstrup several times in the second chapter, "Creation and Ethics: From *Ordnungstheologie* to the Theology of Revolution."

The third chapter is entitled "Creation and Theology: Theology between Dogmatics and Analysis." In this chapter I do not look towards the continent but confine my attention to Sweden, or at least to Scandinavia. The philosophy that dominates Scandinavian universities is the English brand of analytical philosophy. One effect of this philosophy on theology has been a definite negativism toward every attempt to make a total description of Christianity. Theologians in the Nordic countries analyze individual texts by individual authors but are loathe to say anything about what is "Christian" in general. One often suspects that general descriptions of this kind hide a veiled confessionalism. The theologian selects one of the confessions, his own, and labels it alone "Christian."

During my discussion of analytical-philosophical theology I have further cause to make use of Løgstrup's most recent works, and in that connection to deal with my recurring theme, the first article of faith.

The fourth chapter is shorter than the preceding three and is essentially confined to certain practical conclusions. I raise the question of cooperation between Christians and non-Christians in solving common social problems, a cooperation which is only understandable in the light of the first article. In addition, I consider briefly and critically exploitation of nature, pollution of the environment, and similar topics closely connected with the article that concerns the creation of the world. That the church has remained silent about these important points for so long is also a consequence of "The Flight from Creation."

GUSTAF WINGREN

Creation:

A Crucial

Article of Faith

Creation: A Crucial Article of Faith

My Selection of Topics

At the university, when one writes about something, one is closely questioned about the evidence for the statements made about the subject. The reason for choosing to write about that particular topic is seldom submitted to such close questioning. It is usually sufficient to say that the topic has not yet been dealt with. But I wonder whether the choice of topics, often and in many disciplines, is not the most interesting question at the university level. One's whole personality, childhood, youth, and environment have a part in that choice.

Youth

To explain my own selection of topics, I must go back to my early years when I decided to become a theologian, the years of puberty, about 1925-26. In the small manufacturing town where I grew up no one had ever become a theologian; in my family there was no theologian, nor even anyone who had matriculated at the university. The lack of integration, the feeling of discord, was an essential part of adolescent distress. There was nothing to link together the facts of eating, singing hymns, playing football and going to the cinema. Sexuality and the sordid fact of women giving birth to children were forgotten pieces of reality when one played the violin or sang in the choir, I thought. And in the cheerful enthusiasm of the popular movements, death was completely ignored. All the culture and civilization I came across in my surroundings seemed to me to be a flight from reality, escapism. Religiousness was included there, too. One was converted and shook off certain habits. But life was not integrated by piety. On the contrary, religiousness was still only a specialty, one among all the others.

In this situation I suddenly discovered that the actual church building was the only integrating factor. I remember particularly the ringing in of the Sabbath on Saturday, after the clatter from the factory had stopped and before the accordion music of the dance-pavilion began. Here was something that encircled everything from birth to death. The curious thing was that I did not think of this building as religious. I cycled to the rural parishes round about, went to the churchyards, attended morning service and thought that life was one entity. But if anyone had asked me if I was religious, I would have answered no.

A curious adolescent discovery about human actions contributed to this. Some actions were related to the church building. Someone stretched out a helping hand in sickness and death, took care of a boy who had gone wrong, assisted a girl who had become pregnant. These actions seemed to be integrating; strength emanated from them. They were almost always performed by people who had no ideas, people without a plan for their lives. They were simply there and they stepped in when something went wrong.

This has been a long introduction but it is necessary in explaining my choice of topics. I have always sought to choose topics that throw light on the integrating function of the Christian faith in human life as a whole. For this reason I have felt that the modern tendency to cut the church off from ordinary human life is the most profound theological tragedy of our time. The beginning of this constriction lie deep in the rise of pietism before the beginning of the 18th century, but the famous "new consciousness" of theology about 1920 gave fresh inspiration to those who wished to raise high standards round the church. I began my theological studies in 1929 and became a licentiate in 1939 during the most difficult period of constriction, when almost all discussion in theology was aimed at showing the gulf, the discontinuity between Christian faith and human life in general, "the special nature of Christianity," as the phrase went. Of course a young man in his twenties, under the influence of those around him, was drawn into this movement and I had a feeling of being dragged along against my own intentions. After becoming a licentiate, I was in charge of a parish for a time.

Early Theological Studies

But my choice of topic for my licentiate's thesis, presented in September of 1939, was an open door into the future. Irenaeus and Marcion were compared in this first work of mine, which was subtitled "studies in the area of creation." Some of these studies were published in *Svensk teologisk kvartalskrift* 1940 (pp. 133-155, and 322-339). There were three central concepts: the creation, the law, and the incarnation (salvation). The subject matter of my licentiate's thesis came up again in fresh form in 1958 in the book *Skapelsen och lagen* (*Creation and Law* 1961).

In 1958, however, the historical source material for my systematic theses about belief in creation had increased considerably. Irenaeus was certainly still included even at the end of the 1950s, just as he had been the principal figure in 1939-40, but Luther had been included in the selection of material as well. For I had observed early that the subject of my licentiate's thesis did not lend itself to further development. From the point of view of source criticism, Marcion, although a great man, was unusable. After some hesitation, I abandoned the second century and the fathers of the church and moved on to the 16th century and Luther. But it was still the idea of creation that I wanted to deal with. It was the given assumption for all my work. The point on which I fastened finally was Luther's doctrine of vocation, that is, of everyday life and occupations as the place for the Christian to serve his neighbor. To Luther the point is not the discontinuity between a Christian's deeds and the ordinary actions of his work; it is not a gulf but just the opposite. It is continuity, the connection which is the vital point. Underlying the whole of Luther's argument is the conviction that God is the Creator who is still creating life and who, in doing so, uses intercourse between man and woman, the act of birth, suckling one's young, seedtime and harvest, the everyday round.

Into the midst of all these earthly things, the incarnation comes breaking in: *Deus incarnatus,* from whose crucified body spring the sacraments; baptism, which involves all the limbs of the church in daily death and resurrection on everyday ground; Holy Communion with its bread and wine, the provisions for the journey on the way to death and eternal life.

Those years of the early 1940s when I was reading Luther's tremendous cascades of words in the Weimar edition still remain in my mind as a time when I felt as if I were bathing every day in a refreshing lake. This was how my first book came to be written in 1942, *Luthers lära om kallelsen (Luther on Vocation),* which made me an associate professor.[1]

Then I went back to the subject of my licentiate's thesis, eliminating Marcion completely, and decided to make a purely monographic, immanent study of Irenaeus. The central concept here was "recapitulation," that famous "restoration" which plays such an important part in Irenaeus' dispute with the gnostics. To Irenaeus, salvation is not a breaking away from natural life but rather a liberation so that one can be natural, be a human being and re-enter the free "ruling" of the world, its creatures and things. Man is born into this free sovereign state but he loses it when he rebels against the Creator. It is Christ who restores man and gives him back his health, a work of salvation which is now going on in the church. The church cannot be described unless its positive relation to the external world outside the church can also be described. There is a distinct and very fundamental connection between Irenaeus' idea of restoration and Luther's idea of vocation.

Substituting for Barth

The title of the book about Irenaeus suggested itself: *Människan och inkarnationen (Man and the Incarnation)*, completed in 1947.[2] In mid-April, the very week the book was published, I flew to Switzerland to act as deputy professor at Basel in place of Karl Barth while he was lecturing as visiting professor at Bonn. I stayed in Basel until the end of July, lecturing on *Schöpfung, Menschwerdung, Vollendung*, giving seminars on *Luthers Lehre von den zwei Reichen* and suffering all the agonies of the inexperienced teacher. In my seminars I had talented young students from ten nations, Barth's international audience in other words. The whole of my scholarly training had consisted of working with the history of ideas using old sources. At Basel, a historical theme was an uninteresting theme, from a theological point of view. The audience was interested in biblical theology. This did not mean exegesis about the meaning of the scriptures in relation to conditions at the time they were written, but theological theses about the meaning of the scriptures as the Word now being preached.

I could not find any objective reason for rejecting the young Barthians' attitudes towards the question, nor have I been able to find one since. Asking a theologian to answer a question about the meaning of the Word now being preached is as reasonable as asking a lawyer at the university to answer questions about the meaning of a legal text as the law is now being practiced. The meaning in modern times is not identical with the meaning when the law was written down because the prevailing social conditions have altered and hence the meaning of the legal text has also been modified. A historian of law by himself cannot solve problems of interpretation for the benefit of his colleagues in the faculty of law: the other branches of jurisprudence also have contributions to make. Nor can an exegete solve problems of biblical interpretation for the other branches of theology. Exegesis can make a historical contribution to the question but it can never be more than a contribution. A quantity such as "the office of the clergy in the Swedish church" is as new and unfamiliar to the scriptures as the quantity "organ music." When the exegete starts asserting that the Holy Word has something to say about such things he has already gone beyond the limit of the purely exegetical task.

This became obvious to me in Basel in the summer of 1947. It was not the students' attitude toward the question that was at fault but my theological education. I had to admit this to myself when time and again I left my seminars on Wednesday evenings feeling spiritually shaken. But this was only one side of the matter. The other side was an equally clear understanding of Barth's failings. This understanding had to do with the content of what Barth maintained was the essence of the Bible, the incarnation. The modern negation of the belief in creation has Karl Barth as its spiritual father: all others are secondary and have grown up in his shadow. What I had been searching for in Luther, in Irenaeus, was of course a biblical truth too. But it was a biblical truth denied by Barth. Barth is defined by his reaction to liberal theology and its idolization of man. At the very beginning he hurls the Word against "man," a position from which he never escapes, however much he tries. It must be possible to adhere to the belief in creation, to the continuity between the human and the Christian, to the view of salvation as a restoration of the natural and at the same time make room for what is justified in

Barth's position—the interpretation of the Bible as direct address, as the Word now preached.

These ideas decided the subject of my book *Predikan (The Living Word),* published in September of 1949.[3] The index contains many references to two departed writers, Luther and Irenaeus; otherwise the references are principally to Bible passages and to living writers. This is typical and quite intentional. What I was looking for as a young man, an interpretation of the Christian faith which integrated the human element, has no better representatives during the two thousand years of Christian thought than Irenaeus and Luther. They both lived in situations in which the unity of creation and salvation was threatened—in the second century by gnosticism, in the 16th century by the medieval "double morality"—and both of them confined their activities to straight-forward interpretation of the Bible against this threat. To neither of them was creation or the law the main point. Both viewed Christ's death and resurrection as the obvious center. But this center, which coincides with the content of the gospel and the sacraments, is interpreted by both, admittedly in different ways, within a framework of creation and law in which all men on earth are assumed to live. Salvation is a deliverance to naturalness, to essentially worldly duties, already given to everyone in the creation but lost by rebellion against God. These are the simple keystones in my book *Predikan,* written in a mood of some arrogance and sometimes in anger, I admit.

The authorities pondered long about whether the author of this book could be made a professor, but I was appointed to a chair in Lund in the spring of 1951. I do not know whether the appointment was correct— I never took part in the discussion. But having become professor, I was able to go on working. In the summer of 1950 I had again been a visiting professor in Western Germany, this time at Göttingen, where I studied Bultmann.

As soon as I had been given a permanent post in Sweden, I became involved in time-consuming tasks in the world ecumenical movement. For me this meant a new world, mostly Great Britain and the USA. In the course of the years, I visited England and Scotland about ten times and the USA four times, apart from all the other trips I made. Gradually I saw the continent of Europe from the outside in a new way. My travels brought home to me the fact that world theology today is dominated by what happened *on the European Continent after 1920* (this is noticeable particularly in the dazed debate around Bishop Robinson in recent years). The need for a settlement with the methodological currents in present-day European theology was to determine the pattern of almost everything I wrote in the ten years following my appointment to the chair at Lund.

Later Studies

Negative criticism characterized *Teologiens metodfråga (Theology in Conflict)* 1954, my first book of the fifties.[4] In it I discussed three European theologians — Barth, Bultmann, and Nygren — who have dominated as methodologists since 1920 when they gained recognition. Throughout the book my question concerned the problem of where "the fault" in their constructions lie. There must be faults since all three want to render and explicate the content of the Bible and at the same time cut out important sections. Once more it is creation and the law as a framework for preaching the gospel that are lost. Once more it was the inner positive relation of the church to the world I could not find. Personally I am convinced that this book dating from 1954 has a future. It has not yet been read seriously by anyone except those who are already supporters of Barth, Bultmann, or Nygren.

But we are approaching a situation in which these three systems dating from 1920 are losing their influence. It is quite obvious that in the seventies we are experiencing a breakdown of the theological methods introduced into the European universities after the First World War. But those who are rebelling on the world scene of theology do so without settling anything. In the Bonhoeffer renaissance "the world" has suddenly become a beautiful word and "the church" a dirty one, but no one ever tries to make completely clear what is meant by saying that the world is *created* by God. Instead people talk about Christ being before us in the world. We are to "go wheresoever he may be found." Thus the world is interpreted in terms of the incarnation. The first article of faith is omitted and we start at the second—precisely as Barth did. Even worse is the talk at present about "the latent church" and "the church manifest": the latent church is to be found in our society on earth and is thought to be ethically better than the church manifest, that is, better than the congregation celebrating divine service. But the idea that according to Christian belief God has always ruled and still rules his created world by means of *the law,* and that he can do so even without the help of the church, is very difficult to make plain. In imagination, people are stuck at the church concept like the hen to the chalk line.

What theology calls for is in fact a separate analysis of such terms as "creation" and "the law." But this analysis will not be carried out as long as we are tied down to the methodology of the earlier period. For this reason, during the fifties, I organized my writing in such a way that I first wrote the negative and purely critical book on Barth, Bultmann, and Nygren and then two positive accounts, one about creation and the law and the other about the gospel and the church. Both books—*Skapelsen och lagen (Creation and Law),* published in 1958, and *Evangeliet och kyrkan (Gospel and Church)* in 1960 [5]—are based largely on biblical material, from both the Old and the New Testaments, interpreted in the light of the early church and the Reformation. I use the same uncomplicated building materials as in all my earlier writings. It is my intention to repeat these basic theses as long as I can, for they have not yet achieved their purpose.

As regards "creation and the law" particularly, I have the impression that certain non-theological cultural factors on the European Continent are a hindrance. First, the term *Schöpfung* was misapplied in Germany during the epoch of national socialism when concrete theories about "race and blood" were given a theological justification based on the idea of creation. Many Europeans even today cannot hear the word "creation" without thinking of these theories. At the bottom of this aversion to the idea of creation lies, I suspect, Søren Kierkegaard and his hatred of everything that smacks of everyday life, his hatred of all natural forms of life (it was Kierkegaard's ideas that were used in dialectal theology during the 1920s, and in the 1930s against national socialism).

Second, there is the modern variant of the Roman Catholic theory of "natural law" which is used, as a rule, in an attempt to conserve and defend existing economic and social conditions. No wonder quite a number of people in our time have become allergic to the term "law" (this was noticeable during the conference on social ethics in Geneva in July, 1966). This mood means only that we must wait and be patient.

My book *Creation and Law* of 1961 lends no support either to race theories or conservative doctrines of natural law. We must be patient and wait until calm and collected readers can study a positive analysis of these central biblical terms. The Vatican Council is demolishing the traditional doctrine of natural law so efficiently that the field will soon be open, ready for the construction of a new doctrine preferably more biblical than the previous one. The Old Testament contains much material, also, used by the church fathers, that is relevant to this problem.

Even in our more provincial Swedish debate I believe that the model with "creation and law" on the one hand, "gospel and church" on the other, is a necessary and systematic one. The discussion of questions bearing on general morality has been chiefly conducted by Swedish churchmen without the schools of theological ethics in Uppsala and Lund becoming involved in the dialogue. I have been urged several times to take part but so far I have refused to be enrolled as a soldier in the war which morality is waging against immorality in Sweden. I fear the debate is being presented in a way that is theologically wrong. If the church rushes in, Bible in hand, to give an opinion on insemination, abortion, the marriage of divorced persons, euthanasia, and such matters for which there are regulations in the laws of the country that apply to all the citizens, the scripture will be seen as a legislator making demands on the citizens. But if we make law the result of the scripture, we are failing the Bible. Christians should undoubtedly take part in public discussion of the laws of society: they ought to take part far more than they do. But they should do so as *citizens*. Their arguments in *these* questions should start from the common desire of *everyone,* i.e. the citizen's best. When it comes to such questions of legislation one should not use the scripture. The law that is passed concerns everyone, non-Christians and Christians alike.

If the church wants to confess her Lord she does so much more clearly and with a considerably stronger magnetic and attractive power by making known *the joy* she possesses. Present-day life has so little joy that one is surprised to come across it. One cannot help searching for its source. The church can stand back and it can give. We do not have to use the rights which general legislation affords us if we do not wish to: they are not a prey that we must all seize for ourselves. The word of the church to people is a word telling of a gift it has received: it is the word of the gospel and not the word of the law. If the church, besides confessing Christ by word of mouth and in song, wishes to do social deeds, it has plenty of work to do. There are low-paid foreign workers, drug addicts, the handicapped, girls who have been refused an abortion, old people who are lonely—the world is full of people who are despised. Soon the rigid education-minded state will have given us a new group to be scorned, great in number and threatened by bitterness from within—those who did not have a sufficient number of credits to climb higher up the school ladder. In such a society there is only one remedy, only one integrating type of action—voluntary service, voluntarily taking up the tasks which the climbers abandoned.

This service is the classical picture of the church in

the world. Its model is Christ humbling himself as a servant, according to Phil. 2:5-11, the main text in my book *Gospel and Church* (just as the words in the creation story about the rising Adam were the main Bible text in *Creation and Law*.)

The concept of a church totally centered on *the gospel* also predominated in the work of Einar Billing (1871–1939), to whom I devoted two booklets in the 1960s, *Demokrati i folkkyrkan* ("Democracy in the National Church") 1963, and *Folkkyrkotanken* ("The Idea of a National Church") 1964.

In 1968 I finally competed a long-planned work on Einar Billing,[6] the most original of all Swedish systematic theologians of the 20th century and the outstanding figure in Swedish church life even today. "Exodus" was a central concept in Billing's view of the Bible (based on the Old Testament) and in his view of the church (based on Luther). I am convinced that Einar Billing has something to say in our situation today too, although most of his writing was completed by 1920, when Aulén and Nygren took over.

Speaking of Sweden generally, however, the subjects we choose for our theological books may one day stand as monuments to the listlessness of our time, I'm afraid. Large expensive books about topics without importance; slim occasional volumes about vital topics in the center of discussion. It is not easy to imagine a group of doctors in which the professors are authors of books about the Black Death and old-fashioned methods of blood-letting, while the general practitioners on the other hand have written about cancer and polio, since the latter have a practical side that upsets the scientific perspective. Our theological writings in Sweden unfortunately look rather like this. This is the difference between Germany and Sweden. Today the question of the purpose of systematic theology is not a fitting topic of conversation in Sweden unless one asserts that dogmatics is impossible scientifically speaking—in that case one is quite presentable. There are signs, however, of a coming change in the climate.

Finally one more point about my selection of topics. Anyone who, after hesitation, has selected a topic and consequently limited himself knows only too well how many important topics, not finally selected, very closely border on the subject he *did* take. A theological concept such as "natural law" really cries out for a purely philosophical analysis. The task is there waiting but I pass it by. My excuse is that, despite many years of searching, I have found no philosopher, neither analytical nor existential, whom I could take over directly. I am not capable myself of constructing a philosophy from the very foundations.

I can only hope that the topics I leave aside will be dealt with by other writers. What Løgstrup at Aarhus has written in recent years seems to me, even by international standards, to be among the most interesting works in this field, the border country between philosophy and theology. Whether his construction holds, philosophically speaking, I cannot say. But it is worth studying. Løgstrup's analysis of Kierkegaard from the standpoint of the history of ideas is important. The consequences of the analysis extend much further than may appear at first sight. Løgstrup's criticism of Kierkegaard so far is most clearly expressed in a book published in 1968, *Opgør med Kierkegaard (Argument against Kierkegaard.)*

Creation

and

Ethics

Creation and Ethics

From Ordnungstheologie to the
Theology of Revolution

Twice within a lifetime, international problems of social ethics have suddenly thrust themselves on theology. *Ordnungstheologie* emerged at the beginning of the 1930s, just before 1933. The theology of revolution began to take shape in the mid-1960s and spread all over the world after the conference in Geneva in 1966. On both occasions one can rightly speak of a tearing start. The problems did not develop slowly within theology but were hurled at the theologians from outside with an explicit demand for a prompt expression of opinion.

This means that on both occasions theology has had to give its answer without preparation. This lack of preparation is at the core of the problem. What was said about *Ordnungen* in the 1930s and about revolution in the 1960s admittedly is of some interest, too. But

more interesting by far is the fact that theology twice
has been forced to move from its own problems, which
the general public does not care about, to problems
that have grown up in society. There was never time
for the opinion expressed to be based on lengthy research or detailed analysis.

Ordnungstheologie

When *Ordnungstheologie* became established—1932
may be said to mark its recognition — theological
ethics in Europe were based on an idealistic philosophy
with the individual and his conscience at the center.
Kant played an important part in one way or another.
Some people talked about the categorical imperative:
others about the independence of ethical judgment.
But ethics had little to say about *society*. Historical research on Luther was in full swing but interest centered
persistently on his doctrine of justification by faith and
closely related subjects like Christology and doctrine
of the sacraments. There was no way opening out from
these subjects to social ethics, on either the philosophical or the theological side.

If in retrospect one now reads an account so fundamental to *Ordnungstheologie* as Emil Brunner's *Das
Gebot und die Ordnungen,* published in 1932, the most
striking feature is not the systematic working out of
the concept of *die Ordnungen* (orders) in its entirety
but just the opposite: the *Ordnungen* have been *tacked
on.* The whole is complete when the long section on

die Ordnungen (pp. 273-551) is added. And when the whole is being constructed, the term "creation" is comparatively unimportant. First comes, in the accepted manner, the inevitability of the ethical question, the different types of philosophical ethics, and the "contradiction" in which man is placed because of the ethical demand (first section, pp. 1-38). Then comes the gospel, justification by faith alone (which is the motivation of the good), and a definition of the special nature of Christian ethics (second section, pp. 39-94). After that there is a long part on *das Gebot* (commandment), still without *Ordnungen* (four long sections, pp. 97-272). Admittedly, the concept of *Ordnungen* is touched on in this context but only to be demarcated from the "kingdom of God" (pp. 192-203).

What Brunner has given so far is the normal scheme for the dialectical theology of the twenties. After that comes the appended section *die Ordnungen*—279 pages on marriage, work, culture, economics, the people and the state and the church. It is only then, in this added section, that the term *Schöpfung* (creation) takes on significance as a principle (cf. the index). To devote some space to the church at this point fits in well with Emil Brunner's general outlook on the church, in which loosely organized groups are the best expression of the primitive Christian type of congregation, while the church as an institution belongs in the same class as the state and culture (incidentally, this odd grouping of Brunner's is passed on to other writers, where it does not fit in so well). Apart from such a detail, it is the sudden and mechanical tacking on of the idea of creation to the completed structure, in which philosophy and the gospel are the main materials, that is the most conspicuous feature.

Dialectical Theology

We find the same picture in Rudolf Bultmann, existentialist philosophy plus kerygma, that is: philosophy as the framework, the second article of faith as content within the given frame. Basically there is not much difference in Friedrich Gogarten, who published his *Politische Ethik* in 1932, the same year Brunner's *Ordnungstheologie* came out. The total view developed by the group around *Zwischen den Zeiten* in the twenties was a theology built round the second article of faith. Belief in creation was suppressed or neglected. The crucial theological and philosophical factor was probably the Kierkegaard renaissance.

The need to introduce a national ethic or a view based on a principle of *Volk* was then—at the beginning of the 1930s—a need imposed from the outside, not one that grew naturally from within.[1] Many writers were forced to take up social ethics—among others, the group of theologians who had hitherto been connected with the periodical *Zwischen den Zeiten*. Since its members reacted differently to the political pressures, the group broke up. Those who wanted to work up the growing public interest in people and state as a rule used the term *Ordnung* and a mechanically appended first article of faith or idea of creation, without any root in the earlier Kierke- gaardian method of construction.[2]

It is true that in Germany national socialism sup- ported a race ideology that made use of the categories in the creation belief. If we were to mention the names of the theological writers who accepted these race theories about the superiority of the German na- tion, however, probably only collectors of curiosities would prove to be familiar with them. Not even today do we know much about the authors of theological pamphlets supporting race ideologies in South Africa and the USA—these writers are simply adjuncts of the political leaders. The *Ordnungstheologie* of the thir- ties, on the other hand, is a phenomenon found among reliable theologians, whose work is frequently built and structured without resort to the concept of *Ord- nung* and without any very obvious elements of the idea of creation, generally built and structured long before the thirties. By abruptly adopting these new terms, *Ordnung* and *Schöpfung,* they were simply at- tempting to seize on an idea that the public was talk- ing about. They tried to give a theological answer to a question of the moment, a fairly quick answer.

It is also true that in Germany, as elsewhere, there was a conservative Lutheranism which for centuries had distinguished between creation and salvation.[3] The German *Ordnungstheologie* gained support from this quarter too. It is often this contributory support that one thinks of and talks about in looking back to the thirties. If this conservative Lutheranism had stood alone, it would certainly have helped to uphold the political regime by its passive submission, but without any consequences for international theological debate. Emil Brunner and Friedrich Gogarten were pioneers as early as 1932, i.e. before the Third Reich had been established. And both writers had belonged to the dialectical group around *Zwischen den Zeiten*. They were basically alien to conservative Lutheranism. It is *their* fresh approach which was internationally significant. The literary products from Erlangen came later and made use of a stock of terms which then appeared radical and hardly conservative.

Those who held their own in the old dialectical group were Karl Barth and Rudolf Bultmann. Neither of these two adopted the term *Ordnung* in their language and neither of them stated who "the people" were (they did not use the term "Volk"). When World War II was over, these two dominated international theological debate both in Europe and the USA. Bultmann is an exegete and never really touches on social ethics. Barth on the other hand, although still faithful to his Christology, began in 1945 to construct a doctrine of *Schöpfung within* his Christology. The start comes with a conventional enough presentation of Genesis in *Church Dogmatics III:1* and then runs on quite consistently in several volumes of dogmatics in subsequent years. Christology is always the source; social ethics is based on the second article.

The gospel is in principle the *first* word, from which the law—the "second" word—is derived. A very good summing up of the political consequences of this total view is to be found in the little booklet *Christengemeinde und Bürgergemeinde,* 1946.[4]

As an example the following may be mentioned. In the New Testament Christ is called "the light of the world." A government policy which is to take the consequences of this at the lawmaking level should, according to Barth, remove all secret diplomacy and let all international negotiations take place openly in public. In the Christian community, moreover, "the endowments are varied." A political implication of this is that power in the secular society should be distributed among as many people as possible. The Christological line of reasoning seems almost ridiculous in these circumstances. Many people arrive at the conclusion that open diplomacy and distribution of power are the answers without bringing in Christ at all, simply by applying arguments of suitability. But a program based on common sense goes admirably well with the first article of faith. Man is created with "reason," whether or not he is Christian.

Theology of Revolution

Almost 20 years later, in the summer of 1966, the epoch-making conference on the church and society was held in Geneva. It was preceded by four volumes, all published in 1966: *Christian Social Ethics in a*

Changing World, Responsible Government in a Revolutionary Age, Economic Growth in World Perspective, and *Man in Community* (in all 1,542 pages). Several things have happened since then, including the conferences at Zagorsk, Beirut, and Uppsala in 1968. Following these conferences attempts have been made to bring out reasonable reactions, answers, and standpoints from theologians or churches. As more time passes, 1966 will probably stand out as the year of original achievement, the dividing line. But the 1966 meeting in Geneva is not the fruit of theological, or philosophical, or exegetical wrestling with a problem that has developed from within. Both in the four preparatory volumes and at the conference, the social scientists, the economists, and the politicians dominated the whole. They were thrusting a problem on to the church and theology from outside, the problem of "revolution" or "change." "Change" is the key word.

Now comes the basic question. In the 20 years between 1946 and 1966 did anything happen in theology that *prepared* the theological writers to give a considered answer to the question of how "change" or "revolution" in society should reasonably be judged from a Christian point of view? The debates which have been conducted and the theological literature that has been produced in various parts of the Protestant world have touched on this question to only a very slight degree. In some cases the debates and the literature have treated such irrelevant questions that a number of responsible people now feel abashed when one merely enumerates the subjects of that period. On the other hand, what has meant something from an international point of view is the German literature that emerged triumphantly from the crisis in the church on the fall of the Third Reich in 1945. This literature determines almost entirely the way in which the problem of "revolution" or "change" is treated in the wake of the Geneva conference of 1966.

Belief in creation is thus left aside; it is considered to lead to the glorification of existing regimes, to the status quo. This in fact was the function of the mechanically appended term *Schöpfung* in *Ordnungstheologie* during the Third Reich. To Luther, writing in the 16th century, the term *Schöpfung* or *creatio* had an almost diametrically opposed function. It was then the main instrument in society, in worldly matters for supporting and motivating continuous mobility, change, and flexibility. "Equity," or *Billigkeit, Stundelein,* "the mastering of all laws": these are all derived from the idea of creation in Luther, because the emphasis falls on *re*-creation, not on *Ordnung.* But the distortion of the belief in creation that *Ordnungstheologie* brought about in the 1930s is apparently considered even in the 1960s as a true fruit of the first article of faith. If that is not so, why do people recoil so abruptly from the vocabulary of belief in creation? It would be reasonable to start intepreting the first article of faith in different ways so that change and renewal were contained within it. But this does not happen. Misinterpreters have been allowed to keep—quite arbitrarily—the text they misinterpret.

Instead the theology of revolution takes refuge in the second of the three articles. From Jesus and his gospel comes the change in the "structures," the structures of society. Roger Mehl expresses what most of the others assume when in one of the volumes prior to Geneva he clearly makes Christology a fundamental of social ethics. On no essential point does Mehl differ from Barth, who wrote 20 years earlier.[5] The contributors to the work in Geneva in 1966 who disagree with the general view do not influence the subsequent discussion; far less do they modify the planning of attempted solutions. Quite the contrary: the force of the great Christological main theme is strengthened by sporadic voices being raised in objection on the periphery only to be drowned and silenced.

A Different View: K. E. Løgstrup

It is easier to realize the special nature of a certain genre of literature when it is juxtaposed with something totally different. An appropriate object of comparison is K. E. Løgstrup's published work, which ever since his doctoral dissertation of 1942 has dealt with the idea of creation, and which for all these years has concentrated on general human and social problems. He is notably uninterested in the things that theologians discuss—the church, and the sacraments. He is an exception, someone who is prepared to work out what "change" in society might reasonably mean. His voice is not heard in the flow of words from Geneva: it does not blend with the chorus. But he fits in as little with *Ordnungstheologie,* where the idea of creation was a mechanical appendage. In Løgstrup the very basis of the idea of creation is mastered, as may already be seen in *Den erkendelsesteoretiske konflikt (The Conflict in the Theory of Knowledge)* 1942. Consequently, in *Den etiske fordring (The Ethical Demand)* 1956, he starts out from a general human phenomenon, the dialogue (and the confidence a dialogue implies), when he attempts to establish the import of the silent and unspoken demand that every human being as a human being is already faced with.

For this reason the idea of creation does not lead on to *Ordnungen* in Løgstrup. In his work of 1956 he comes to the relationship between the sexes *(Den etiske fordring,* first ed., pp. 87 ff.), to the relation between society and property (pp. 104 ff.), to the process of secularization (pp. 111 ff.). In the very headings of these three sections Løgstrup talks in an almost stereotyped way about one and the same thing: the change (three times he uses the same Danish phrase, "de sociale normers foranderlighed illustreret med . . . . ", pp. 87, 104, 111, and also 77). But in the midst of his discussion of the relativity of all social norms and conventions, Løgstrup retains his starting-point, the idea of creation and the radical demand. It may be admitted that Løgstrup is difficult to read. I have had difficulty in understanding him myself and at one time unjustly grouped him with Gogarten.[6] But the lines of thought summarized here are as clear as daylight and no one can mistake them. By his flexibility he differs from *Ordnungstheologie* and by his heavy emphasis on "change" he shows a certain affinity with the theology of revolution that suddenly burst into the open in the sixties.

But it is typical of Løgstrup that he first describes the normal, the kind of existence in which life goes on much as usual. He does not take a leap straight into change as do so many other theologians. An operation in the hospital or shock treatment undoubtedly means an intervention which can completely revolutionize a person's condition. There are surgeons who have theories about operations but none of them builds a theory directly—without first having an elementary anatomical and physiological theory about what a body is and how a person normally functions. That sort of "ontology" is now prohibited in theology for various reasons, theological and philosophical. Løgstrup has ignored the prohibition, and it would probably also be worth while for others to ignore the prohibitions, posing the problems that should be first considered, problems raised by but ignored in their own work.

The question of what it means to be a human being is undoubtedly a more important theological question just now than that of revolution or "change." The general anthropological question is logically superior. "Change" must be something secondary as a principle. And Løgstrup's latest book *Opgør med Kierke-*

gaard (Argument against Kierkegaard) 1968, gets to
the root of the problem of the twenties and its Kierkegaard renaissance, more than any other comparable
present publication. We are all—at every theological
level—influenced by what happened when Kierkegaard was relied on to draw the line for what "Christianity" meant and when at the same time a number of
working methods developed which are being used in
theology even today, undisputed. These methods make
it quite simply impossible to ask certain necessary questions and they impede fresh treatment of some central
biblical material—among other things, the idea of creation. That is why *Schöpfung* became a dead weight in
1932; that is why flexibility disappeared from the outlook on society in *Ordnungstheologie;* that is why the
critics of *Ordnungstheologie* sought refuge in the second article of faith; that is why motivations for revolution or "change" are now drawn directly from Christology and the gospel. To argue against Kierkegaard
as Løgstrup does is social ethics. It is basic research in
social ethics.

Christology and Social Change

Why is this important? Why should anyone tear to
pieces the fashionable link between Christology and
revolution?

There are good reasons for adopting the radical opinion that the centers of our cities should be closed to
motor traffic and left free for pedestrians and cyclists.
Those who want to travel in greater comfort to the

city center would have to use public transport—bus, underground, or tram. Several young radicals maintain this view and I share it absolutely. However, I would not want to derive my opinion from Christology —although I believe without the slightest doubt that my fellow-men and service to my neighbor would benefit by drastic measures against the nuisance of motor traffic. For the moment I shall ignore the fact that I do not have a car, that I like to walk, often go by bus and happen to own a bicycle. Even these details (which are perhaps common to me and several other radical opponents of cars) make it conceivable that "the old Adam" may have something to do with my radical opinion. But these are comparatively unimportant points of view. The main point is that those who oppose my opinions—those who plead for the free spread of traffic in the city center—have many humane arguments on their side: the old and the handicapped can get right to the shop door, and so on. It is just as easy for them to derive their thesis from Christology.

From an objective viewpoint, neither my opponent nor I gain anything constructive by basing our reasoning on Christology. In fact we definitely suffer several factual losses. In the first place, we contaminate the gospel, each of us in his own way. It is now confined to *one* side of a social conflict. In the second place, we decrease the scope of our argument. We argue in a way which is empty and pointless in the eyes of citizens who are atheists or followers of Islam, but who have the same right to the city center as we have. They may of course accept our points of view for other, empirical or social reasons. But then it would be more correct factually to try and track down those other reasons. After all those reasons can carry some weight with all men, whatever their faith, assuming that it is really a *social* question we are discussing and not an ecclesiastical one in disguise.

This is where we touch on a core point. Confronted with *Ordnungstheologie* and the theology of revolution one may feel the same kind of uneasiness, uneasiness that the social commitment is not genuine, not absolutely genuine. In the last few decades in Europe the ecclesiacentric interest within theology, interest in the church and questions of how it is to cope, have dominated so much that it would be a sheer miracle if such a persistent germ were to die.

If it were true even today that the prestige of the church is the only concern, that and not social questions, then unfortunately everything would logically correspond from beginning to end, from 1932 to the present. Then *Schöpfung* must be appended about 1932, must drop off in 1945 and later be avoided; then "change" and "revolution" must be added on about 1966—naturally with reference to the second article (since the first is supposed to advocate national socialism!).[7] A devastating perspective opens up. If this were true, it would mean that there is not a serious word in the theological work of the period—everything would be simply an echo of the struggle for power in the world. It is to be hoped that only a few theological writers think in terms of prestige and that the work as a whole is produced because certain factual problems have developed from within as necessary.

One such necessary problem from a factual viewpoint, one that theologians can no longer evade, is the question of what "create" and "creation" signify. Some people may perhaps think that the parallel between revolution in a developing country and overcoming the tyranny of cars in a European city is a lame one. It is true that there is a great deal dividing the two phenomena. But if one tried to enumerate the things that distinguish them one would find that revolution is— if possible — something even more "worldly" than measures against the tyranny of motor cars can ever be. If it was obvious from the above reasoning that one should not involve the gospel in arguments for or against certain measures concerning the centers of our cities, then it is even more obvious that one should not motivate revolution by referring to Christ's gospel. In some cases one can argue for revolution in an objective way without resorting to the New Testament for support. But it is quite certain that one will cause great harm by making Christ a supporter of revolutionary groups. He can be used for this purpose as little as he can be used to support existing regimes, the status quo.

Creation and Life

Here the key biblical terms "create" and "creation" come into the argument. In classical theology, the idea of creation is not used as a means of introducing Christological arguments into social debate but just the opposite: the gospel argument, by means of the idea of creation, is brought *out* and the common sense arguments of suitability are brought *in* in the debate. Governments, of course, consist of people but despite this they are often actually put in the same class as fields of rye, apple trees, and biological phenomena, that is, natural phenomena. One may thank God for apple trees and regard the harvest as a gift from him. After rational consideration, one can also cut down apple trees and clear the land, thanking God for air and light and fresh opportunities for cultivation. Neither when one lets the trees remain standing nor when one cuts them down does one judge the steps taken as "Christian" or "un-Christian"—it is an irrelevant approach to the question, a way of reasoning that we are released from by belief in creation.

Masses of actions which people have performed over the centuries are independent of the Christian faith in that they were carried out in the service of life by Christians and non-Christians alike. These include caring for one's child and working for one's living. Within this simple, primitively biological sphere, people can communicate with each other using elementary common-sense arguments, and can see eye-to-eye at this level. The gospel does not add anything new to our everyday store of knowledge, and yet the actions within our everyday spheres are not situated beyond the scope of God; on the contrary, they are gifts of the

Creator of the same type as rain and sun. The Old Testament is instructive here. The point of its texts is not that the peoples round about Israel have knowledge of Jahweh the true God. But that these peoples are alive is a daily gift from the true God—him whom Israel has learned to know, and to whom they sing praises in their worship.

If one turns to the Old Testament to seek some indication of a "natural revelation" one will find only scanty material. If one seeks indications that God gives life then the material is abundant; in the Psalms, in the Prophets, in the historical books, everywhere. The early church had a good biblical basis when, in opposition to the gnostics, it made the first article stand on its own feet before the article about Christ and the article about the church. If Judaism or Israel was driven into a nationalistic course during its history, then the idea of creation—to which *inter alia,* Deutero-Isaiah bears witness—is the most implacable criticism of all such constrictions: Jahweh is God of the whole world who accomplishes his dominion even if his own people must perish. If a particular people in Europe in the 20th century used the terminology of the creation belief to assert "Aryan" race theories for what are clearly national-socialist ends against other peoples, then it follows that the only reasonable theological conclusion is this: now we must be more thorough and explicit in talking about what "create" and "creation" mean. We must now really *analyze* the meaning of belief in creation.

The result has been reverse, as we know. Theologians have fallen silent about the matter. If there had been an interpretation of "Christianity" that was directly hostile to the Old Testament idea that God gives life and gives it to all, to heathen and believers alike; if there had been an interpretation of "Christianity" that was hostile to natural manifestations of life; then that interpretation might be a true explanation of the theological history of the last few decades. National socialism's misuse of the concept is no explanation. Taken by itself it gives instead good cause for a more detailed and exhaustive account of what "create" and "creation" mean. A more conceivable explanation for this failure is Kierkegaard, besides others. Throughout his life he fostered aggressions against the belief in creation just indicated. To him "Christianity" was a breaking away from natural manifestations of life, a break with what "one" does.[8]

Down here, in a tangle of problems which developed before the 1930s with their political unrest; down here in typically erudite writings, we must look for the real problem that both *Ordnungstheologie* and the theology of revolution have wrestled with and tried to solve. That is why analysis is now more important than commitment. With the demand for commitment one forces people to leap straight into already established groups formed on purely political lines in our earthly society. The theological arguments for that sort of choice of positions are nearly always rationalizations. As one puts greater distance between theological work and such commitment, one's line of argument on social questions should become more objective as we have just seen. But one also gains in clarity on the theological side in the quiet of the study where the analysis is to be made. One must be at a distance in order to see.[9]

There is another benefit to be gained, a third, that can be obtained by putting distance between theology and political commitment. When the gospel, which is the basis of the church, ceases to be a motivation for concrete political measures, the church regains its universal task in relation to all different kinds of people, independent of their grouping in society. It would be disastrous for the mission in developing countries if the gospel was confined to one side of the conflicts. On the horizon of Europe, *Ordnungstheologie* in the 1930s seems to be a national twisting of people's interests and the theology of revolution an international expansion of them. But Africa and Asia show strange combinations of revolution and violent nationalism. . . . [10] The conflict between Nigeria and Biafra is a signal here. It cannot be fitted into an ordinary scheme of "left" and "right." Other conflicts of similar kinds may arise, this time supported by strong elements of Christian revolutionary theology on one or the other side. In this situation the church cannot function with the gospel in relation to everyone, not when it has first been committed to one side.

What has been said here does not mean that the gospel of Christ has no political consequences. Christ is a person and he helps people to be natural and to see what common sense requires of them. This is no new knowledge of a supernatural kind. The same clear-sightedness can come to one in a situation that is filled with hate and quarrel if, for example, a little child suddenly appears who is not full of hate and who is raised above that which the adults are fighting about. To see what is natural is difficult—one needs a helping hand, a "catalyst," to see it. But it is the natural things that one sees, that one has always known deep down. In this way the gospel picture of Christ gives us a push in the same direction as "nature," the creation. His picture compels us to *change* the conditions of our fellow men as best we can.

The permanent function of the church in relation to everyone, independent of social groups, does not come out when one looks at the church from the point of view of social ethics and looks for her achievement in changing our social structures. However, it may be illuminating to know that questions about the results achieved by the church in society touch only one sector of her task. It cannot be assessed as a whole from this sector. In this the church differs from a political party. One can form an opinion of a political party as a whole when one has seen its program for society.

Creation

and

Theology

Creation and Theology

Theology between Dogmatics and
Analysis

First of all, a definition of the three principal terms is necessary. If one considers it a reasonable task to give the general outline of a "theology" which strikes a balance between "dogmatics" and "analysis," a great deal is already assumed. "Dogmatics" on the one hand and "analysis" on the other are both apparently inadequate. It is impossible to stick to one of them without running into difficulties. One must make one's way between them and set up new positive tasks for this subject called "theology."

If we start with the term "theology," I should like to propose that this term—as distinct from the science of religion in general—be defined as the scholarly work which, on the basis of historical sources, aims to state what is characteristic of the Christian faith and the Christian ethos as compared with other kinds of religion and philosophy in our times; to state what is "Christian" in a descriptive way using scientific reasoning, i.e. using arguments which can be tested by everyone.

Further, I propose that the term "dogmatics" in our context be taken to mean the normative process by which the truth of the Christian confession of faith is upheld while that faith is described scientifically. When one describes Islam, one does not contend that Islam is the truth. Nor does one exclude the degree of truth of Islam. Theology can leave questions of that kind out of the actual description. But it is typical of "dogmatics" in its earlier accepted sense that the normative assertion of the truth of the Christian faith is an integral part of the actual description.

In our time the science of religion, working analytically, has dissociated itself from this kind of dogmatics. This dissociation has led not only to the decline of the normative propositions in theology but also to certain other consequences which are neither necessary nor desirable from a scholarly viewpoint. The description of Christianity as a totality is threatening to disappear entirely as goal for analysis. In the New Testament it appears that one can pass considered judgments on the thoughts of Matthew, John, Paul, or Luke, but descriptions of the early Christian faith as a whole are said to be historically impossible. In the later history of ideas, analyses are made in a similar way of Lutheranism, Presbyterianism, or Thomism. Attempts to say something about "what is Christian" are on the whole dismissed, often as being veiled confessionalism or a late instance of normative dogmatic thinking.

Strangely enough, at the same time comprehensive judgments may be passed on such complex phenomena as Islam or Buddhism without any apparent scruples in spite of the fact that these religions are also divided into various factions and extend over thousands of years with varied historical forms. The scholarly prohibition against comprehensive descriptions laid down by rigid "analysis" applies, it seems, only to Christianity. Precisely here, comprehensive descriptions are the same as "persuasive definitions." If one talks about "the Christian faith" in general, then one is found guilty of spreading the same kind of propaganda as the politician when he talks about "true democracy," "genuine freedom," "healthy nationalism."

I propose that we call this negative scholarly attitude toward any total view of Christianity "analysis." This means, then, that "analysis" like "dogmatics" in its earlier sense suffers from a defect. "Dogmatics" is deliberately and openly normative. "Analysis" not only rejects this deliberate normativeness but also rejects the unconscious or veiled normativeness that it sees concealed in the guise of comprehensive description. Since we have already defined "theology" as the scholarly work which tries to state what is characteristic of the Christian faith and ethos, it is quite obvious how we look upon the topic given: "Theology *between* dogmatics and analysis." It is a matter of achieving comprehensive descriptions of the Christian faith and ethos without falling into the normative patterns of dogmatics.

Methodology and Creation

I have dealt with just such a definition of tasks in my previous work. In a way it is the main problem in my book *Teologiens metodfråga* 1954 (*Theology in Conflict*). I would like to modify the presentation given there, however.

To start in the actual impulse behind the preaching now going on is an approach I still find rewarding and correct. The biblical text is not a text in the past alone but is a text expressed now, through the act of preaching, to an audience whose situation is a totally different situation from the situation of the people in the early Christian congregation. Preaching is only one example. In teaching, in divine service as a whole, in prayer, everywhere, biblical texts are always being brought into the situations in life of new people and these situations are inserted into the texts themselves, filling the words of the texts with new and unexpected content.

For instance, one might consider the meaning of the prayer "forgive us our trespasses, as we forgive those who trespass against us." The content of the words for every individual praying, and every day that passes in the course of the centuries, is quite new—and at the same time quite concrete, without a trace of abstraction. But what is new and concrete is not subjective or an arbitrary invention. It is quite the reverse: the variation, the constant alternation is intentional when the prayers in "Our Father" are uttered for the first time. But the same is true all the time, as long as the Word functions. Change and continuity do not cancel each other out. The correct interpretation of the Bible, the one that is faithful to the past, must constantly contain change. To maintain the status quo is to lose continuity.

I still believe that this idea is correct. It is the fixed point, and, to future theology, an indispensable point in the re-orientation of the 1920s on the Continent (Karl Barth, Rudolf Bultmann, and others) that should be maintained. In Sweden, this re-orientation has had practically no importance, which is a loss to Swedish theology. To some extent it has been compensated for by the renewal of interest in Einar Billing, which has come at long last. Billing, whose theology was born out of the crisis brought about by biblical criticism, developed as early as 1907 an essential part of the substance later contained in the continental kerygma theology.

But some modification is still needed, both a correction of Einar Billing and a fresh approach in relation to everything that I have written. It is my conviction that the work of K. E. Løgstrup, the Danish theologian, is helpful along this line. His writing, ever since his doctoral thesis of 1942, has consisted of uninterrupted reflection on the possibilities of making clear to people today what the Christian faith involves.[1]

In Billing's theology, Exodus takes precedence over Genesis. God's election of Israel is interpreted but

God's creation of man and the world receives no explanation. His theology deals with the church but lacks anthropology.[2] I attempted to correct this in my books *Theology and Conflict, Creation and Law,* and *Gospel and Church,* but my correction was made in the form of a rather superficial analysis of the "multitude of demands" (German *tatsächliche Forderungen*). Very rapidly I moved from creation to *the law*—and to that concrete law, the demands that are actually made on us from outside in our relationships with our neighbors. From the preaching of the gospel one can not, I argued, primitively derive new laws, but one can surely do some "sifting" (German *Sichtung*) or "screening" among the "multitude of demands."[3]

There is some truth in this and I shall return to it presently. As a correction to Billing these attempts of mine are sufficient. But as positive expressions of what "creation" means they are totally inadequate. I believe that Løgstrup's work can take us further. In my opinion, Løgstrup has identified more clearly than any other contemporary theologian the assumptions in the 1920s, showing them to be results of the Kierkegaard renaissance and also of a conscious and deliberate nihilism that up until now has had a devastating effect on every attempt at a positive anthropology. Since 1920, every thesis that has interpreted constructively what "man" is in the light of the belief in creation has been destroyed. Against any such positive thesis, Christology or the catchword *Offenbarung* (revelation) has been set. This is a typically Kierkegaardian argument. In Kierkegaard Christ is really an impediment to the natural manifestations of life. Løgstrup argues that this view is in conflict with both the Old Testament view of life and Jesus' preaching, and he states his arguments with increasing emphasis and explicitness every year.

In this context it is of great interest to see that analytical and existential philosophy appear as children of the same spirit. It is customary to set these two up against one another. On Scandinavian soil, analytical philosophy dominates, Englishmen and Americans being cited as authorities. In Germany, it is quite the reverse. There theology often relies on the very philosophers that Scandinavians reject; Heidegger and those who are more or less influenced by Heidegger. I am convinced that in time both will emerge as typical philosophies of the individualism of the western world about the mid-twentieth century. The individual choosing freely without any objective grounds is at the center of both. That which is called "evaluation" in analytical philosophy is called *Entscheidung* by Heidegger. In both cases it is asserted with a curious kind of frenzy that the individual's choice is subjective, that no theoretically establishable norm can be placed above the individual's act of choice to guide it.

Whichever of these two philosophies theology allies itself with, the result will be the same. The idea that man is created and that his life is dependent on the Creator—the same Creator who rules the world—that idea must be disowned. It means that anthropological nihilism is the actual foundation on which Christology, the doctrine of the church and related subjects is "placed." The greater the force with which these great quantities (Christ, the church, revelation) are postulated, the more nihilistic theology will become— and the more "worldly" it must also become! The church quite logically will actually be, as Karl Barth says directly, "the leading political entity."

In his profoundly sophisticated reasoning, Løgstrup maintains that there are definite conditions under which life can be lived and other conditions under which life is inexorably harmed. These conditions, he says, can be noted, observed, and described. Some are of an ethical nature. They consist of certain attitudes that people do or do not adopt. One of these is "trust" between people. I will not summarize what Løgstrup says about dialogue and about people's way of "putting their lives in the hands of others." Of particular value in his work is the combination of two things that often diverge. He manages to combine a radical, immutable demand with a striking relativization of all moral and social conventions. In his thought the mutability of norms, paradoxically enough, is the result of the constancy of the radical demand. Since the radicalness in the demand is permanent, the norms change from time to time.

Løgstrup performs this most elegantly in his analysis of the development of economic life from feudal times to the present day. Medieval society was built on privilege. The knight paid no taxes but he lived under the pressure of an ideology which demanded courage in war. He enjoyed privileges so that he would protect the defenseless. When after the French Revolution the liberal society abolished the privileges of the nobility, the bourgeois ideal of free competition was introduced instead. The pauper and the previously privileged would set out from the same position; everyone would start on equal terms. But it soon became apparent that people have different capacities for earning money. In the new capitalist system, private property and wealth were not placed at the service of the poor as in medieval society. Thus the socialist society, with high taxation of incomes, had to follow the liberal society. And there we stand today. In this development the conventions changed. But the driving force behind the changes was always the same, constant, radical demand: the care of the weak.

Løgstrup seems to me to have hit the mark on these central points. That is why I now find my own start in the "multitude of demands" during the years 1954-60 rather superficial and poorly thought out. In my reasoning from that time I can now find traces of nihilism.

But in trying to achieve a doctrine of creation, one must also of necessity put a question mark after the term "Christian ethos." As the idea of a specifically Christian ethos is developed in the theology influenced by Barth (e.g. in N. H. Søe), it is quite clear that the actual basis of the system is deliberate nihilism. "Conscience" is mentioned in the New Testament, to be sure, but Søe asserts emphatically that conscience in itself is absolutely empty of content—it is given content from outside by absorbing historically given types of ethos. The good has some latitude in the conscience on only one condition, namely that the Word fills the conscience with meaning, with "the revelation." Søe presents an unusually well-reasoned nihilism in his ethics; only a few writers have carried reflection as far as he has. But in principle one comes across the same nihilism in other quarters at present, indeed wherever people when faced with a concrete moral problem think that they must "look it up in the Bible" in order to get an answer. And that attitude is very widespread on the continent of Europe.

It is important I think to observe that this attitude is new. It is practically unknown before 1900. In all earlier theology account is taken of a natural law, a universal law, whereby God as Creator forces even heathen to give service to their fellow-men in society. This idea of a natural law received its death-blow as late as 1934 (the Barmen synod) although nihilism, which then definitely triumphed, had of course long been prepared, at any rate since the 19th century especially through pietism and Kierkegaard. If one disregards these modern misdirections and keep to the classical forms of the Christian faith, one must put forward certain theses that may seem surprising at first sight.

Creation and Christian Faith

By way of introduction I talked about "the Christian faith and the Christian ethos" as the objects to be described by theology. On very good grounds one ought to be able to say that the Christian faith can be correctly described only by saying no to an exclusively Christian ethos. The Christian faith, since it is a belief in a God who is God of the whole world, assumes an elemental ethos of a universal kind; it assumes rules for man's co-existence with his fellows which are quite simply there and functioning as long as life continues. On the other hand belief in Christ is determined by the fact that Christ by some form of "word" has become known. Faith comes "from preaching," as the phrase runs—and "preaching" may very well take place by reading a text, or by looking at a crucifix, or nowadays, a film.

The human universal ethos which we are dealing with here has developed in the history of mankind. It is not timelessly given. Today almost no one will openly admit that he is opposed to freedom of speech but one can date the origin of this idea historically. For quite a long time, it was believed that people had full freedom of conscience even when there was no right to public self-expression. In those days, e.g. in the 16th century, no one was ashamed to openly proclaim himself an opponent of free speech. Only later on did it become known that a person is deprived of his humanity when he is prevented from speaking out.

In this sense, Christ and the New Testament can be the source of a great many ethical stances with universal applications. Among them are attitudes toward children and the sick. Everyone wants to care for the sick and support helpless children. This demand is often expressed more strongly in socialistic, atheistic countries than in the old bourgeois, traditionally Christian societies. It is conceivable that historically the positive interest in children and in the sick was first formulated in the New Testament. But this means only that Christ reveals what is "human"—it is then human and universally human. Everyone, even atheists and opponents of the gospel, recognizes after this disclosure the universal naturally given ethos (which many people of course violate, just as members of the church have broken the commandments in the Bible over the years). The fact that Christ has historically brought to light many ethical insights does not mean that the insights today must be taken from the proclamation of Christ by the church.

On the other hand in the New Testament there is another "word" which comes from Christ, a word that cannot be formulated as a commandment or an order for human co-existence, a word that cannot be accepted or become an object of belief unless Christ is raised to a level above all mankind. It is the phrase "Thy sins are forgiven thee." If anyone has offended *me,* it is human for me to forgive this. If, on the other hand, I go up to a person whom I have never seen before, who has not done anything to me personally either good or bad, and say to this stranger, "Thy sins are forgiven thee," then I am behaving as Jesus Christ did according to the Gospels. If the picture given in the Gospels of Jesus of Nazareth is historically correct on this point, and from a historical point of view there is no reason to doubt it—then such a historical person is either mad or God.

The church takes the risk of asserting the latter.[4] The words about the "forgiveness of sins" which the church preaches are the very heart of "the gospel." This word, the specific word of the church, works on the assumption that the whole world "comes under the law." The idea of a universal ethos, a "natural law" is not difficult to combine with the idea that the church has a specific, a *unique* word to preach. On the contrary, these two points go together very well.

But the important question, the difficult question, can be phrased as follows: Does the preaching of the gospel not have consequences of an ethical nature? Is there not an effect arising from the preaching of the gospel that is re-creative and changes the universal general human ethos, since its content—quite independent of the church and Christianity—is subjected to historical growth, development, change?

To this question, on which Karl Barth in his day excelled by making all sorts of ingenious statements, Løgstrup gives scarcely any answer at all. Barth, of course, using analogies from Christology and from the New Testament, could show the necessity of, for example, open diplomacy between nations and the distribution of power within nations. Løgstrup deals with how creation "cures itself," and he has little to say when one asks him what Christ and the New Testament have meant for the development of society. Barth's enemy is *Deutsche Christen* and his theme is *Evangelium und Gesetz* (gospel and law). Without the revelation in Christ, according to Barth, human life is an ethical vacuum, a nihil. Løgstrup's enemy is Kierkegaard and so his thesis is the doctrine of "the supreme manifestations of life": trust, charity, general humanity without which life cannot be lived. They are given, they are there before our decisions—and if they are not given we cannot create them by acts of the will. When one tries to bring about joy or love one sees how dependent one is on gifts. The elemental human quality, that which lends life value, is always given. It is there before our decisions. It is creation.

But the words unique to the church, "the forgiveness of sins," are a typical gift. If anything lacks the nature of an act of will or a decision on our part, it is the forgiveness of sins offered to us by the gospel. Would this gift not create something new in human social life? Forgiveness is ethically re-creative even by the very fact that it wipes out and breaks down. What it breaks down is barriers that prevent a spirit of community, guilt barriers. Forgiveness is at its very purest when no audible word about forgiveness is uttered but the whole of life in society instead testifies that the earlier wrong no longer exists.[5] It is a fine anthropomorphism full of deep wisdom when the Bible sometimes describes God's forgiveness as his forgetfulness, "He no longer remembers." This miracle that human life is swept clean by the fact that one "does not remember" is one of the most powerful re-creative ethical forces in existence.

Forgiveness in this sense, forgetfulness, makes ordinary human life possible again, even though it may be practically impossible to achieve by nature. Perhaps the human phenomenon, forgetfulness, is exactly what the world needs. This forgetfulness may even be a consequence of Christ's forgiveness. The misery, the lack of unity, the dissent in mankind is essentially due to people everywhere "remembering" and never "forgetting." They never get a fresh start, never manage to come down to the pure "original state" again, Adam's state before the fall (to use the old mythological vocabulary used by the fathers of the church in their doctrine of creation). The church could be a return to unspoiled humanity by its preaching of the "forgiveness of sins."

Løgstrup's quietness about this reflects a gap that is connected with a certain absence of reflection about the destruction of human life. He makes apt remarks about "the supreme manifestations of life" and about their character as given phenomena, "before us": they are earlier than our decisions, we get them. But in the same way, the destruction of our life is given before us. The hatred of adults for each other surrounds the sleeping infant who will one day waken to a life of which hatred is already a part. Before the individual himself has decided to be envious, envy has ruled the individual's family. We do not decide on wickedness, but we "get" sin. Our own individual sin is in fact before us. The destruction of life is given, just as the supreme manifestations of life—trust, joy, love—are given.

Discussion of "original sin" has been trivialized in western tradition by being confined to the sexual act and the idea of a biological heritage. But one can equally well interpret "original sin" in terms of social psychology. There is a realistic observation behind the old assertion that evil is given before all our decisions. But that side is rarely a subject of reflection in Løgstrup, a fact which is connected with his enemy being Kierkegaard, who one-sidedly cultivated the original sin idea. Therefore Løgstrup—just as one-sidedly—brings "the supreme manifestations of life" to the fore. They were completely ignored by Kierkegaard.[6]

In this lies the justification for using the terminology taken over from Luther that characterizes of my own work, principally during the years 1954-1960. The Christian "screens" the multitude of demands coming from those around him, he "sifts." God's will to create takes effect in the demands my neighbor makes upon me. These demands—in the midst of their humanity —are God's law. But since destruction is implicit in all that my neighbor demands of me, I must "sift" and "screen" these demands: there is hatred, envy, sheer arbitrariness in them. The preaching of the gospel is a critical principle in handling the mass of demands that actually surrounds us in our contacts with our fellowmen. This is the moment of truth in Barth's doctrine of God's law as derived from the gospel.

Quite a different matter is the Barthian thesis that man without Christ lacks knowledge of the good. By taking that view, one starts in anthropological nihilism, in an ethical vacuum. And where there is a vacuum there is no sense to such terms as "sift" and "screen." If we are ever going to understand afresh the older classical theories about a "natural law," then we must, I think, shelve questions about the degree of knowledge man possesses independent of the gospel. It is by no means self-evident that this question of knowledge should be at the center of the debate. There are certain possibilities for life to be lived and for its rules to function, even if man has no theoretical knowledge of the content of the rules. This is a key point in Løgstrup's discussion of "the supreme manifestations of life": they are at hand and function before our reflection on them.

If one makes the question of knowledge the principal question, then that which is given by Christ, the gospel, is also transformed into a question of knowledge. The doctrine of how faith arises becomes a sort of specific theological theory of knowledge. It is odd that this is what happened to Karl Barth, who wanted to stimulate theology to greater respect for the special nature of the Bible. The picture of Jesus given by the three synoptic gospels is dominated by two things: the statement about the forgiveness of sins and the healing of the sick. All the blind, the dumb, and the crippled are given their health again quite simply— and are also given forgiveness, which from one point of view is health too, a return to the state of man before destruction. If someone who has been burdened with guilt and crippled is freed from guilt and given the ability to walk, it is an arbitrary theological procedure to subsume the "newness" given by Christ under the heading "Revelation to him who is ignorant by nature." A heading like this does not come from the Bible.

In fact we need a "theology of the synoptics," centered on the image of Christ as the forgiver and the healer and we need a construction of the church at present which conforms to this "theology of the synoptics." Grundtvig in Denmark and Billing in Sweden are a beginning.[7] Neither of them has had any great influence on the Continent, where Søren Kierkegaard is looked upon as the only Scandinavian worth listening to.

A "theology of the synoptics" with the starting-points mentioned here would not have to be put into contrast with Pauline or Johannine theology. With his development of the great basic contrast, life-death, Grundtvig is rather Johannine in his interpretation of the miracles of healing. And Billing, who bases everything on "the forgiveness of sins," can work out the whole of his ecclesiology by exegesis of Paul's doctrine of justification by faith (thus e.g. in his work *Försoningen,* 2nd ed. 1921). Both Grundtvig and Billing have had a noticeable effect on the popular conception of life in Denmark and Sweden, respectively. They have also had a democratizing influence on the legislation in their countries. Grundtvig was partly responsible for the abolition of the coercion laws at the municipal level during the 19th century, and for the instigation of the Danish people's high-school. Billing is expressly mentioned in the jurisprudential preparatory work for the Swedish act concerning freedom of religion, 1951.

An integrated New Testament total view, that is, a unified picture of "that which is Christian" on the whole, the subject we specified in the introduction as being a suitable one for "theology" is a perfectly reasonable aim. That this total view is not represented by any one particular present-day confession or by any one particular church in existence goes without saying. They all read the same Bible texts but these texts form a critical authority higher than the interpretation of the text by all individual churches, just as a piece of music constitutes a critical authority higher than all concerts, all attempts to play the piece.

This is a program of work for "theology" but it is not "dogmatics" in the accepted traditional sense. The message proclaimed is addressed to the faith of the listener but the authority of the message does not receive any support from science. The words about "forgiveness" are as easy to push aside as they were when Christ first uttered them. They are just as difficult to believe today as they were then. And so it should remain. Otherwise faith would no longer be faith.

Return

to

Creation

Return to Creation

If one looks at the development of the Christian church from the period before World War I up to the 1970s, one is struck by the fact that during the 1930s and 40s the church closed in on itself while after a few years of hesitation in mid-century it rapidly opened itself up to the world during the 1960s and 70s.

This phenomenon is understandable. The theologically productive country was Germany whose *Bekenntniskirche,* to which both Barth and Bultmann belonged, was polemically opposed to National Socialism, which at that time represented "the world." The term "world" had a negative ring; it was a case of cutting the church off from its surroundings, keeping it and its teaching pure. In the years that followed World War II, the whole situation suddenly changed. The colonial period was over; African and Asian nations began to receive their independence, simultaneously discovering their frail economic situation. Under these conditions, to take on "the world" and jointly shoulder responsibility for secular problems

becomes *Christian,* demanded by love. The term
"world" changes face and becomes something
positive.

When the church was withdrawn into itself, on its
"flight from creation," it was fairly natural to neglect
the first article of faith (this article was directly mis-
used by the racist ideologies of the Third Reich).
But today, fear of the first article is an anachronism.
"The flight" now places theological reasoning in obvious theoretical difficulties. For the social and political program to which churches all over the world
now give their support are often thought out and
presented by persons who are not of the Christian
faith. The church allies itself only secondarily to
worldly manifestos. How then can a program or
manifesto be justified theologically by the gospel, by
the specific words about Christ which the church
alone—not the world—acknowledges?

The new practical situation during the 1960s and
70s should also produce a shift in emphasis at the
theoretical level. But there are no signs of such a
change. This may lead to a very dangerous self-
righteousness on the part of the church. We must
make the effort to understand theoretically how a
person *without* "the right faith" can accomplish things
which benefit his fellow men and which, with respect
to the world, are useful.

The preaching of Jesus is full of examples on this
point. According to the Sermon on the Mount we
should model our behavior towards our neighbor on

the sun, which shines on good and bad alike, and the rain, which falls on both the righteous and the unrighteous (Matt. 5:45). Another model is the Good Samaritan, who didn't belong to God's chosen people, yet stopped to tend a wounded man, neglected by the priest and the Levite, though these two represented in all respects "pure doctrine" (Luke 10:30-37). Examples such as the sun and the rain, the father who gives his child bread (Matt. 7:9-11), the Samaritan and the other, from Israel's point of view, poorly informed people whose knowledge of the biblical commandments was slight if any, cannot be understood at all if one removes from the discussion every mention of God as the Creator, the Father of *all* people, who is able to treat them all as his children. Why in our time this side of the Bible should be hushed up is a mystery.

The gospel differs from the law in that it speaks primarily to the individual. It doesn't deal with our own practical contributions to the state of the world. It has something to say to me, an individual, even when I am about to die and cannot reasonably be expected to do anything at all which may be of benefit to others. A church cannot solely resolve itself into "social action" without failing the lonely, the unwanted and the dying—those who don't even have the strength left to pray or move their lips any longer. Jesus Christ, at any rate, did not fail them. His last conversation with a criminal at the place of execution, Golgotha, brings this out well enough (Luke 23:40-43).

This is not to say that the gospel only talks about "heaven" or "paradise" and keeps quiet about life on earth. The gospel, after all, paints a picture of a person, Jesus Christ. We cannot see this picture without seeing community and fellowship. For that person never did anything solely for his own good—others were always included in his actions. He who today, through hearing and accepting the gospel, receives Christ as a gift, also receives life as a gift. The gospel gives life, natural, human life.

But we had life previously too, before and irrespective of the gospel, even if it was in a perverted and damaged condition. Ethically, the gospel doesn't add anything "supernatural" to our ordinary nature. The gospel cleans up; its clarifies and gives a form—but it gives a form to something which we have already lived in, as people. This simple situation is borne out by an experience which each of us can have whether or not we are Christian. When we neglect to do something good our negligence is almost never the result of ignorance of the good. We knew but we didn't do the good. The gospel doesn't need to give any new ethical "knowledge." It is much more important that it gives us the Lord, who sacrificed his own life to offer everyone who believes the gift of daily fellowship with him.

But these question-marks to the face of modern theology, question-marks that have been advanced for many years, only increase in importance during the 1970s. For our new responsibility becomes more and more a responsibility to nature. In order to protect man, in particular the weak and the stressed, during the coming years we must begin the great battle against environmental pollution all over the world: the fight against industrial poisoning of water, air and earth; the fight against meaningless rise in production which sacrifices the health of the individual for fairly pointless material gains; the fight against a population explosion which can only be halted by a new, conscious respect for the female body; above all the fight against mass hunger. Not one of these new fields can be mastered unless Christians and non-Christians co-operate by using common-sense arguments; not one of them can be touched unless we direct our attention positively to the natural phenomena around us.

Taking on this job while there is a "flight from creation" is inconceivable. In its biblical texts and in its long history, the church has a wealth of thought about God as the Creator. Tragically, these beliefs are neglected, even though the churches' creed, repeated every Sunday, begins:

"I believe in God the Father Almighty, Maker of Heaven and Earth."

Notes

Notes

Chapter 1

1. Philadelphia: Fortress Press, 1957.

2. Philadelphia: Fortress Press, 1959.

3. Philadelphia: Fortress Press, 1960 (paperback, 1965).

4. Philadelphia: Fortress Press, 1958 (paperback, 1960).

5. Philadelphia: Fortress Press, 1961; Philadelphia, Fortress Press, 1964.

6. *An Exodus Theology. Einar Billing and the Development of Modern Swedish Theology.* Philadelphia: Fortress Press, 1969.

Chapter 2

1. Cf. Arvid Runestam's article on "Ordnungsteologi" in *Svensk Teologisk Kvartalskrift* 1937, pp. 125 f., where this point of view is strongly emphasized and rightly so.

2. In Gogarten, however, the actual term *Ordnung* does not play an essential part.

3. On this point, see Henning Lindström, *Skapelse och frälsning i Melanchthons teologi* 1944, pp. 360-403.

4. Cf. my essay in the new compilation *Gesetz und Evangelium* 1968 ed. by Ernst Kinder and Klaus Haendler (pp. 260-276). The essay was originally included in the miscellany in honor of Barth on his 70th birthday, *Antwort* 1956.

5. R. Mehl in "Christian Social Ethics in a Changing World" 1966, pp. 44-58 (against Gunnar Hillerdal).

6. Cf. Løgstrup's reply in *Kunst og etik* 1961, pp. 266-271, esp. pp. 270 f.

7. It should perhaps be added that the English and German editions of my book *Creation and Law* provoked reviews in Germany and Great Britain in which it was said without further ado that to combine creation and universal law is to support national-socialist theories.

8. See e.g. pp. 40-68 on the sacrifice and the disintegration of natural communities in K. E. Løgstrup, *Opgør med Kierkegaard* 1968.

9. This is why Einar Billing and his *Exodus Theology* is of such importance. It was planned and completed about 1920—and then forgotten.

10. This comes out clearly in H. W. Gensichen's lecture on "Revolution und Mission in der Dritten Welt" at the meeting of the Lutheran World Association's Theology Commission in Geneva in August 1968, published under the title *Revolution and Mission in the Third World,* Lutheran World, vol. 16, 1969, pp. 12-28.

Chapter 3

1. A thorough account of Løgstrup's writing and a critical analysis of its problems may be found in a doctor's thesis by Lars-Olle Armgard presented at the University of Lund in 1971 and entitled *Antropologi: Problem i K. E. Løgstrup's författarskap (Doctrine of Man: Problems in the Writings of K. E. Løgstrup.)* The most important of Løgstrup's works in our context are *Den erkendelsesteoretiske konflikt* 1942, *Den etiske fordring* 1956, (later published in several Danish editions and translated into German), and finally *Opgør med Kierkegaard.* Articles and lectures by Løgstrup are to be found scattered throughout a number of publications in various places, both in Denmark and beyond it.

2. Cf. my book on Billing *An Exodus Theology* 1969, in which this thesis is developed throughout.

3. See *Evangelium und Gesetz* 1963, pp. 279 f. (reference word Klärung, Sichtung) and *Gospel and Church* 1964, p. 265 (reference word, Sifting of demands) where reference is made to various passages. In the work *Theology in Conflict* the term "actual demands" is used to translate the Swedish *faktiska krav* (see e.g. pp. 161 f.).

4. "The church is the forgiveness of sins." This is the keystone of Einar Billing's ecclesiology.

5. Once again Billing's ecclesiology is a direct result of his interpretation of the gospel. The church makes no conditions *whatsoever* for the right to become a "member." In this way, in this openness, the church is "the forgiveness of sins."

6. See e.g. *Opgør med Kierkegaard* 1968, pp. 110-116.

7. On Grundtvig, see Harry Aronson, *Mänskligt och kristet* 1960 and Kaj Thaning, *Menneske først* I-III 1963.

Author

Gustaf Wingren is professor of theology at the University of Lund in Sweden. He is internationally known through his writing, his lectures in many countries, and his work with various theological conferences and commissions. Several of his books have been published in English: *Luther on Vocation; Creation and Law; Gospel and Church; Theology in Conflict;* and *An Exodus Theology.*

724
2890